VIOLIN

10 jazz standards and original pieces with play-along CD

Alexander L'Estrange and Tom Pilling

© 2005 by Faber Music Ltd
First published in 2005 by Faber Music Ltd
3 Queen Square London WC1N 3AU
Cover by Velladesign
Music processed by MusicSet 2000
Printed in England by Caligraving Ltd
All rights reserved

ISBN 0-571-52305-6

CD recorded at Wedgwood Studios, Surrey, January 2005
Engineered by Oliver Wedgwood
Produced by Alexander L'Estrange and Tom Pilling
Piano: Tom Pilling, Bass: Alexander L'Estrange, Drums: Mike Bradley
℗ 2005 Faber Music Ltd © 2005 Faber Music Ltd

2

C jam blues Duke Ellington arr. Pilling

C jam blues Duke Ellington arr. Pilling

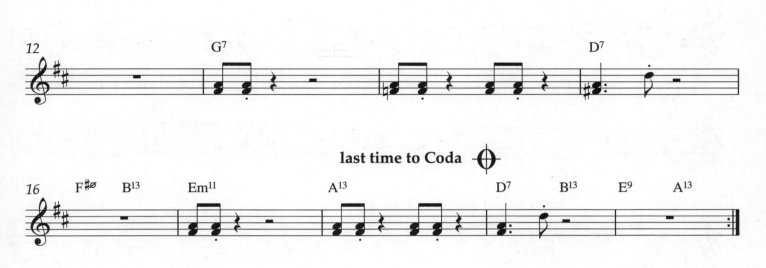

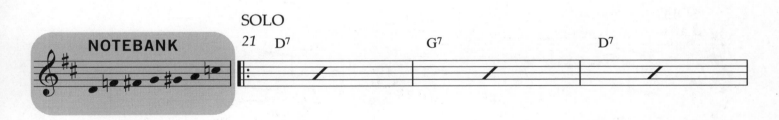

3 Snowdrop Tom Pilling

4 Snowdrop Tom Pilling

Wade in the water traditional spiritual arr. L'Estrange

Wade in the water traditional spiritual arr. L'Estrange

7 Wanna walk with me? Alexander L'Estrange

Wanna walk with me? Alexander L'Estrange

* Play first time only

Fly me to the moon Bart Howard arr. L'Estrange

Fly me to the moon Bart Howard arr. L'Estrange

Song for Jo Alexander L'Estrange and Tom Pilling

Song for Jo Alexander L'Estrange and Tom Pilling

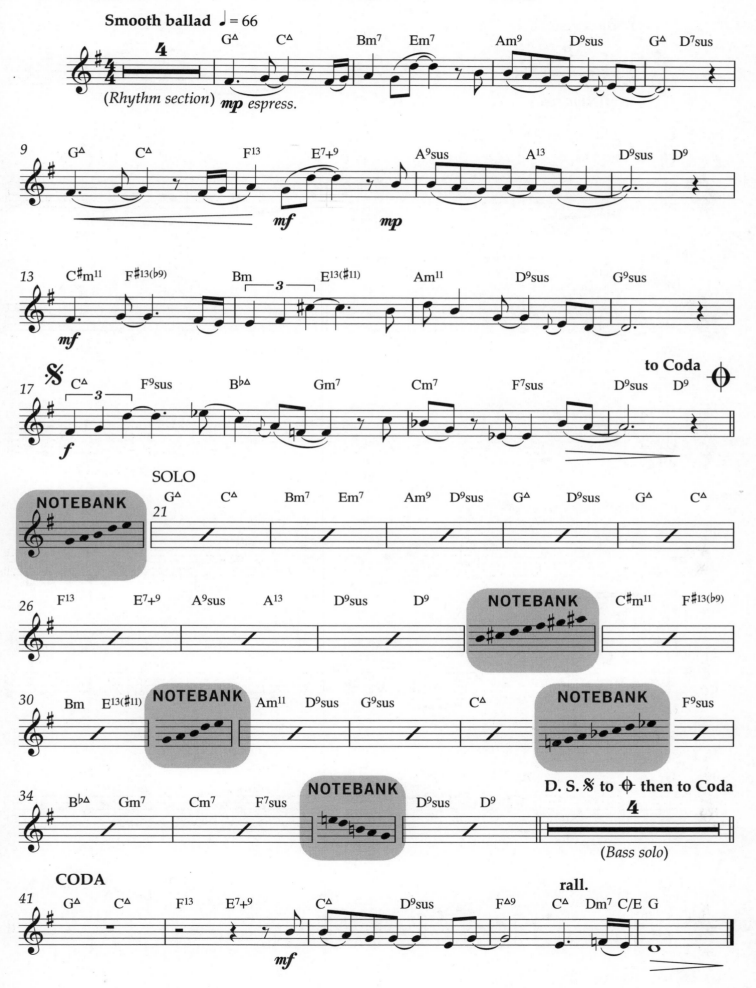

Bradley's bounce Alexander L'Estrange

⑭ **Bradley's bounce** Alexander L'Estrange

16

15 **It's me, O Lord** traditional spiritual arr. L'Estrange and Pilling

It's me, O Lord traditional spiritual arr. L'Estrange and Pilling

17 Hafiz Zahran Tom Pilling

Hafiz Zahran Tom Pilling

Stompin' at the Savoy
Benny Goodman, Chick Webb and Edgar Sampson

arr. Pilling

20 **Stompin' at the Savoy** Benny Goodman, Chick Webb and Edgar Sampson
arr. Pilling

How to use this book

Jazz Sessions is a play-along album with a difference. The CD backings were recorded by real live musicians, so not only do you get to play along with your own band, you can really get an authentic feel for the style. And because improvisation is a key skill for all jazz musicians, each piece in *Jazz Sessions* appears in two versions. On the left-hand page you will find the 'written-out solo' version ready to be played straight through, whilst the right-hand page has a second, extended version for improvisation and experimentation. 'Notebanks' have been included in these versions, to help you get started. Try experimenting with using the pitches in different octaves, and in any order. They are a guide only – of course it is perfectly acceptable to use any of the 12 pitches at any time, as long as they sound right! Experiment with chromatic and whole-tone scales and modes too. When you have mastered creating your own melodies from the suggested pitches, you can then begin to follow the chord symbols.

If you want to develop your improvisation skills further, there's no better way than by listening to as much jazz as possible, and copying and experimenting. The essence of jazz is in exploration, and we hope that you enjoy exploring the pieces in this book.

Alexander L'Estrange and Tom Pilling

Wie man dieses Buch benutzt

Jazz Sessions ist ein "Spiel-mit" Album der anderen Art. Die CD-Aufnahmen wurden mit Live-Musikern eingespielt – somit kann man nicht nur mit der eigenen Band spielen, sondern bekommt auch ein echtes Gefühl für den Stil. Und weil Improvisation eine Schlüsselfähigkeit für Jazz Musiker ist, gibt es jedes Stück in *Jazz Sessions* in zwei Versionen. Auf der linken Seite findet man die einfache Solo Version, bestens geeignet zum Durchspielen, während auf der rechten Seite eine zweite, ausgebaute Version für Improvisation und Experimentieren zu finden ist. 'Notebanks' sind in diesen Versionen enthalten um bei den Anfängen zu helfen. Versuche einfach, mit den Tonhöhen in verschiedenen Oktaven zu experimentieren. Sie sind nur eine Richtlinie – natürlich ist es absolut richtig irgendeine der 12 Tonhöhen zu benutzen, solange sie sich gut anhören! Experimentiere auch mit chromatischen und Ganztonleitern und Tonarten. Wenn man die vorgeschlagenen Tonhöhen beherrscht, sollte man anfangen den Akkord Symbolen zu folgen.

Zur Weiterentwicklung der Improvisationsfähigkeiten gibt es keinen besseren Weg als so viel Jazz wie nur möglich zu hören, zu kopieren und zu experimentieren. Das Wesen des Jazz liegt im Erforschen und Entwickeln und wir hoffen, dass man die Stücke in diesem Buch mit Vergnügen spielt.

Alexander L'Estrange and Tom Pilling

VIOLIN MUSIC FOR THE ESTABLISHED BEGINNER
FROM FABER MUSIC

Up-Grade!
Light relief between grades
PAM WEDGWOOD

GRADES 1–2 ISBN 0-571-51954-7
GRADES 2–3 ISBN 0-571-51955-5

The Young Violinist's Early Music Collection
10 gems for violin and piano
arranged by EDWARD HUWS JONES

ISBN 0-571-51669-6

Position Pieces
*Easy repertoire for violin and piano
in 2nd, 3rd and 4th positions*
edited by MARGUERITE WILKINSON
and ALAN GOUT

ISBN 0-571-51436-7

Got those Position Blues?
*9 jazzy pieces for violin and piano
in 2nd, 3rd and 4th positions*
EDWARD HUWS JONES

ISBN 0-571-51534-7

Gypsy Jazz
*Songs and dances from across
Europe for violin and piano*
POLLY WATERFIELD
and TIMOTHY KRAEMER
EASY LEVEL ISBN 0-571-51637-8
INTERMEDIATE LEVEL ISBN 0-571-51937-7

Jazzin' About
*Fun pieces
for violin and piano*
PAM WEDGWOOD

ISBN 0-571-51315-8

To buy Faber Music publications or to find out about the full range of titles available
please contact your local music retailer or Faber Music sales enquiries:

Faber Music Limited, Burnt Mill, Elizabeth Way, Harlow, CM20 2HX England
Tel: +44 (0)1279 82 89 82   Fax: +44 (0)1279 82 89 83
sales@fabermusic.com   fabermusic.com